CHRIS ROCK

Other titles in the series **African-American Icons**

BEYONCÉ
A Biography of a Legendary Singer
ISBN 978-0-7660-4230-8

JAY-Z
A Biography of a Hip-Hop Icon
ISBN 978-0-7660-4232-2

JENNIFER HUDSON
A Biography of an American Music Idol
ISBN 978-0-7660-4233-9

SEAN "DIDDY" COMBS
A Biography of a Music Mogul
ISBN 978-0-7660-4296-4

TYLER PERRY
A Biography of a Movie Mogul
ISBN 978-0-7660-4241-4

CHRIS ROCK

A Biography of a Comic Genius

Marty Gitlin

Enslow Publishers, Inc.
40 Industrial Road
Box 398
Berkeley Heights, NJ 07922
USA
          http://www.enslow.com

Library of Congress Cataloging-in-Publication Data
Gitlin, Marty.
  Chris Rock : a biography of a comic genius / Marty Gitlin.
      pages cm. — (African-American icons)
  Summary: "Discusses the life of Chris Rock, including his childhood in New York
City, his rise to stardom as a stand-up comic, his family life, and his work in movies and
television"—Provided by publisher.
  Includes bibliographical references and index.
  ISBN 978-0-7660-4229-2
  1. Rock, Chris—Juvenile literature. 2. Comedians—United States—Biography—
Juvenile literature. 3. African American comedians—Biography—Juvenile literature.
4. Actors—United States—Biography—Juvenile literature. 5. African American
actors—United States—Biography—Juvenile literature. I. Title.
  PN2287.R717G58 2014
  792.702'8092—dc23
  [B]
                              2013000127

Future editions:
Paperback ISBN: 978-1-4644-0401-6
EPUB ISBN: 978-1-4645-1220-9
Single-User PDF ISBN: 978-1-4646-1220-6
Multi-User PDF ISBN: 978-0-7660-5852-1

Printed in the United States of America
112013 Lake Book Manufacturing, Inc., Melrose Park, IL
10 9 8 7 6 5 4 3 2 1

To Our Readers: We have done our best to make sure all Internet addresses in this
book were active and appropriate when we went to press. However, the author and
the publisher have no control over and assume no liability for the material available
on those Internet sites or on other Web sites they may link to. Any comments or
suggestions can be sent by e-mail to comments@enslow.com or to the address on
the back cover.

   ♻ Enslow Publishers, Inc., is committed to printing our books on recycled paper.
The paper in every book contains 10% to 30% post-consumer waste (PCW). The cover
board on the outside of each book contains 100% PCW. Our goal is to do our part to
help young people and the environment too!

Cover Illustration: AP Images / Charles Sykes.

CONTENTS

Chapter 1

INSPIRING A COMIC GENIUS

Chris Rock paced the stage like a caged lion. His raspy voice belted out one funny punch line after another. He did not wait for the laughter of the crowd to die down to deliver another hilarious joke.

He was the hottest comedian in America—and he was on fire. Rock was ranting against President George W. Bush and the war raging in Iraq. It was a grave subject. As usual, he was using biting humor to voice his view.

"Bush lied to me. They all lied to me," he began.

It was March 2004. Rock was on stage recording his *Never Scared* show at Constitution Hall in Washington, D.C. The audience was hanging on every word.

"They're like, 'we got to go to Iraq because they're the most dangerous country on earth. They're the most dangerous regime in the world.' If they're so dangerous, why did it take only *two weeks* to take over the whole [darn] country? You couldn't take over Baltimore in two weeks!"

The crowd roared with laughter. Rock flashed his wide, toothy, mischievous grin. His eyes glared into the crowd. The break was just long enough this time to allow the audience to catch its breath. Seconds later, he had them in stitches again.

Rock sees himself as the Incredible Hulk of comedy. He goes on stage and destroys the targets of his jokes. Then, when he becomes Chris Rock again, he cannot believe what he has done.

"Did I just say that?" he asked himself in an interview with noted journalist Charlie Rose. "Oooh . . . that's *mean*."

It was mean. But it was funny. It was so funny that the audience could not stop laughing.

No person or subject is safe from his humor. Rock embraces topics that other comedians are afraid to touch. He jests about racism, politics, religion, guns, and drugs. Joking about such sensitive issues causes some watching him on stage to squirm in their seats. Others might chuckle nervously. Some even blush.

But Rock makes them think. He is unafraid to make light of the most serious topics. His goal is to take subjects that are not funny and make them funny. He hopes that he can help solve problems by bringing them out in the open. He indicated to *New York Times* reporter Cindy Pearlman in 2001 his belief that the ills of society can only be cured if people talk about them freely.

"Yes, it hurts," he said. "But I figure that laughter sometimes starts from pain. You might wince, but then I know that I'm doing my job. The only thing I can do wrong is not be funny."

If his routines make some critics uncomfortable or unhappy, Rock is comfortable and happy. He knows that not everyone understands his brand of humor. He is content to entertain those who do.

Rock has been making people laugh since childhood. He first gained fame when he joined the cast of the famous comedy skit show *Saturday Night Live* in the early 1990s. He later rocketed to fame on stage.

He was soon considered one of the greatest comedians in American history. In 2001, TV network Comedy Central ranked him No. 5 on its list of the

"100 Greatest Stand-ups of All Time." Three of his comedy albums earned Grammy Awards, which are presented annually to the best performances in music and other forms of entertainment.

Rock, however, has never been one to explore just one avenue in his career. Though he could have stayed rich and famous solely as a stage comedian, he sought new outlets for his talent on television and in the movies. He yearned to be a director and producer. It did not take long for him to achieve those goals. He eventually became an actor in a Broadway play.

Rock produced several stand-up specials for cable network HBO that earned Emmy Award nominations. His 1996 show titled *Bring the Pain* captured two Emmy Awards and gained him international stardom. His late night talk program titled the *Chris Rock Show* (1997–2000) also earned Emmy recognition.

His quick wit and ability to joke with large audiences resulted in work as a host of awards shows. Rock hosted the MTV Video Music Awards in 2003, but the best was yet to come. His edgy humor landed him the Master of Ceremonies role at the prestigious Academy Awards in 2005.

Rock set the stage for a wild evening as he arrived to a standing ovation from the most celebrated actors, directors, and producers in Hollywood. But in typical

Rock fashion, he shocked them and entertained them with one cutting remark.

"All right! Sit your [butts] down!" he shouted. The audience roared with laughter.

Rock continued to take his career in different directions. He kept his name in the public eye by writing and cocreating the sitcom, *Everybody Hates Chris* (2005–2009). The show, based on his childhood in the tough Bedford-Stuyvesant section of New York City, earned a Golden Globe nomination.

He soon turned his attention to the big screen. He acted in dozens of roles and even lent his voice to popular animated films for children, such as *Osmosis Jones*, *Madagascar*, and *The Bee Movie*. He has admitted that he is a far superior comedian than he is an actor. But he added that he would like to contribute to critically acclaimed movies and work with the most prestigious directors.

Rock has indeed searched for new avenues for his talent. But he has remained intent on creating laughter on stage. He has refused to tone down his message. Yet the anger and aggressive nature he displays in his routines does not represent his offstage personality. Rock is funny away from the spotlight, but he is also pleasant, shy, and quite serious at times.

"I have my own demons and dark moods," he said. "It's weird. I kind of keep my personality in my pocket a lot. When I start to do stand-up, that's not my true personality either. It's the personality of a guy who hasn't been able to say what he wanted to say."[1]

And Rock has wanted to say a lot. Among the subjects he has embraced as fodder for his routines is race relations, one of the most controversial and sensitive topics in America. He is unafraid to joke about it. He is happy to express his opinion on any social or political matter. Sometimes, he touches on all of those subjects in the same performance.

As the 2008 presidential election heated up, he made it known that he was backing Democratic candidate and eventual winner Barack Obama. He also offered his feelings about President Bush. Rock joked to *Rolling Stone* magazine reporter Bill Zehme that the Republican, who had lost much of his popularity while in office, was making it difficult for future white male candidates.

"Bush has [messed] up so bad that he's made it hard for a white man to run for president," Rock claimed. "'Give me anything but another white man, please! Black man, white woman, giraffe, anything!' A white man has had that job for hundreds of years— and one guy has [messed] it up for all of you!"

Rock maintains a strong awareness of current events and trends. He devours newspapers and magazines. He knows that what is happening in politics and pop culture can be turned into humor. He keeps his routines fresh. The knowledge he gains by staying informed allows him to cater to the interests of his audiences.

But Rock is not motivated to keep up with the news simply as a comedian. His interest is genuine. He is fascinated by the world around him. He soaks in every political shift or social change. And when anything dramatic occurs, he knows how to transform it into humor.

"The times compel him, and he processes it as only he can," said friend Bill Stephney, who helped form Public Enemy, a popular American hip-hop band. "His mind and eyes should be donated to science. He doesn't really know the gravity of his own power. It's sort of like the Olympics with him. Every handful of years, there's a Chris Rock moment."

Rock was not the first comedian to explore grave political and social issues. He was not the first to show his anger or express his views in his routine. He was not the first to use profanity on stage. He was greatly influenced by comedians who came before him and allowed him to achieve success. He used what he learned from them to develop his own style.

Among the first was a fellow New Yorker named Rodney Dangerfield. Rock told television interviewer Jonathan Ross that he considered Dangerfield "probably the funniest guy to ever walk the earth." Rock has little in common with Dangerfield as a comedian. Dangerfield, who died in 2004, did not touch on political or important social matters. But Rock marveled at the passion Dangerfield felt about stand-up comedy.

Rock was also inspired by two troubled and tragic figures in the recent history of comedy: Richard Pryor and Sam Kinison. Richard Pryor, also African American, was ranked by Comedy Central as the greatest stand-up comedian ever.

Pryor suffered from severe depression and died at age sixty-five. Rock learned through him that even the most sensitive topics were fair game. Pryor influenced Rock to take risks on stage when delving into topics, such as American race relations. Rock said he considered Pryor to be the king of comedy.

Rock also enjoyed the shouting style of a short, frizzy-haired white comedian named Sam Kinison, who gained fame briefly in the early 1990s. The son of two preachers, Kinison simply raged at his audiences on stage. Rock was impressed that Kinison blazed new trails in comedy and expressed brutal honesty. Rock also embraced the heavy use of profanity that was a Kinison trademark.

Rock is no clone of any comedian. He shouts, but does not scream at the top of his lungs like Kinison.

He does not whine for effect like Pryor. Rock walks back and forth on stage, stopping only to deliver the punch line with emphasis as he stares into the crowd. The line is often followed by a mischievous smile and glaring eyes that scream out, "Am I right?"

He is happy that his audiences are color blind. He believes that they do not care about the ethnic or racial background of any comedian. They only want to be entertained.

"People basically aren't that racist," he told media icon Oprah Winfrey in 2002. "They want their laughs. If I make a white guy laugh, he's gonna come see me. He's not gonna go see the white guy who doesn't make him laugh just because that guy is white. That's why comedy is one of the few [professions] in the world where you can absolutely transcend race."

His audiences react because they are interested in what he is talking about. He understands that he can draw the most laughter if he focuses on topics of greatest concern to the largest number of people in the audience.

Among the most sensitive subjects in recent years has been gun violence. The tragic shootings of youths in the streets and schools has caused anger throughout the country. Rock would never make light of murder. He would never diminish the tragedy. But he expressed the frustration and rage of Americans through humor.

He poked fun at those who claim that rap music and movies are causing such terrible events.

Rock began one routine by claiming he had grown fearful of white male teenagers because of the outbreak of school shootings. He caused laughter by recalling the days when what he described as "crazy" kids were separated from the others. He voiced the feelings of millions of older Americans, who remember when their cities and schools were much safer. And he offered a solution that had his audience laughing hysterically.

"You don't need no gun control," he said. "You know what you need? You need *bullet* control. . . . I think all bullets should cost five thousand dollars. You know why? Because if a bullet cost five thousand dollars . . . people would think before they killed somebody."[2]

But with controversy comes criticism. Black comedian Whoopi Goldberg chastised Rock for his put-downs of celebrities. Rock has also been condemned for his frequent use of profanity. Legendary black comedian and actor Bill Cosby refused to appear on his show, claiming that Rock's frequent use of the word "nigger" contributes to giving black youths a poor self-image.

Critics claim that some of the most successful comedians in the world, including African Americans like Cosby and Sinbad, have kept their shows clean.

Rock has been quick to answer. He has argued that many comedians use foul language in their routines. He added that he uses the "n" word on stage to draw a distinction between educated, motivated black people and those going down the wrong path in life.

"Our young people are using [the word] to justify ignorance," he told Winfrey. "So I pointed out that the people who use the word, people that are embracing the word are truly ignorant. . . . It's not a cool way to live. . . . It's like a lot of young black kids think it's cool to not know things, think it's cool to not follow the law, think it's cool to not behave themselves. That's not cool, that's ignorant. I just felt like pointing out the [ignorance] mentality. It has to stop."

Criticism of Rock over his use of the word stemmed from his stand-up routine titled "Niggas vs. Black People" in 1996. The highly controversial bit was shown in his breakthrough HBO special, *Bring the Pain*. Rock rocked the world of comedy by describing what he perceived as the differences between the two.

"There's, like, a civil war going on with black people, and there's two sides," Rock began. "There's black people, and there's niggas. And niggas have to go."

The black audience roared their approval. But critics complained that Rock was justifying white racism. They claimed that Rock was ignoring what they believed to be the underlying causes of crime in the inner cities, such as poverty and hopelessness. Rock expressed his view on stage that if others in poor black communities could thrive, there are no excuses.

"You know what the worst thing about niggas is?" he asked. "Niggas always want some credit for [stuff] they're *supposed* to do. . . . Niggas will say [things] like, 'I take care of *my* kids.' You're *supposed* to, you [idiot]. What kind of ignorant [stuff] is that? 'I ain't never been to jail.' What do you want? A cookie?"

The groundbreaking routine helped Rock gain fame and fortune. But he grew and learned from the criticism. He later explained in an interview with TV news magazine *60 Minutes* that he discarded the routine because he felt it gave racists the notion that it was all right to use the "n" word.

The maturity Rock has gained as a comedian mirrors his growth as a person. The road from the streets of New York to manhood and stardom was long and difficult. But caring parents and a drive to succeed helped Rock blossom into greatness.

Chapter 2

TOUGH LOVE, TOUGH CHILDHOOD

C hris Rock often uses life experiences to express himself as a comedian. He is so tied to his childhood that his memories growing up in the tough Bedford-Stuyvesant section of New York City spawned his award-winning sitcom, *Everybody Hates Chris.*

But he was too young to remember much about his first home. Rock was born on February 7, 1965, in the tiny town of Andrews, South Carolina. It was a time and place in which racism ruled the South while an era of violence and tragedy was taking hold in the United States.

When mother Rose and father Julius began raising their son, South Carolina was just emerging from the Jim Crow era. The period, which lasted from the end of slavery and the Civil War in 1865 to the mid-1960s, was marred by discrimination against African Americans in the South. Laws impeded blacks from exercising basic American rights, such as voting. Segregation shunned blacks from the rest of society.

African Americans were either separated or banned from public places or utilities, such as restaurants, beaches, swimming pools, parks, bathrooms, and drinking fountains. Black youths attended inferior schools.

The South and the rest of America was changing before Chris was old enough to begin his education. Millions of African Americans demanded change. Civil rights leaders, such as Martin Luther King, Jr., had led a movement to end racial discrimination through nonviolent protest. Slowly, schools and public places in the South were integrated. The 1964 Civil Rights Act and 1965 Voting Rights Act, both of which were pushed through by King and signed by President Lyndon Johnson, provided African Americans with the legal means to rights that had been afforded other Americans for many years.

But more militant blacks, such as Malcolm X, had grown impatient with the pace of change. Inner city blacks across the country who had become tired of discrimination and living in poverty began rioting. From 1965 to 1968, riots in nearly every major city caused the loss of life and property. After King was assassinated in April 1968, violence occurred in more than 120 cities.

The Rock family was growing by that time. Chris was just the first of their seven children. Though the Jim Crow era in the South was mercifully over, his parents were dissatisfied. Despite the legal changes in the South, racism still prevented black people from obtaining the best jobs and equal opportunities in education. Many African Americans had left Andrews and other smaller communities in the South to seek greater economic opportunities in the North. The Rocks became one of them in 1972. They took Chris and younger brothers Tony and Andre to Brooklyn, a borough of New York City.

They rented an apartment in the Crown Heights section of town, but soon bought a small house in Bedford-Stuyvesant. The area is known affectionately as "Bed-Stuy." Rose took a job as a schoolteacher while Julius drove a newspaper delivery truck. They showered Chris with love but demanded a strong work ethic. They even made him responsible for the lives of his family members in the event of an emergency.

"I had a lot of responsibility," Rock recalled to David Keeps, a reporter for men's health magazine *Best Life.* "In case of a fire, I was the guy in charge. It almost feels like I was raised on a farm. I had chores. Get up, put out the bowls for the oatmeal, run the water, put the pot on the stove, pour the oatmeal for the kids. And then at night, it's bath time. 'Okay, Chris, you go run the water again.'"

Rock realized his gift for comedy at an early age. People laughed at him even when he was not trying to be funny, as he explained to Oprah Winfrey in their 2002 interview.

"When I was about six, I said to myself, 'Wait a minute—I'm dead serious and everyone else is cracking up,'" he recalled. "I thought, 'I've got something here. Let me learn how to work it.'"

His first notion was that he wanted to become a comedy writer. He watched the credits roll by at the end of a comedy program and noted the names of the writers. He decided that his name would be among them someday.

Bed-Stuy, however, was not a funny place. It was a tough neighborhood. Many of Chris's friends gave in to temptations. They sold drugs. They stole from stores. They got into fights. But Chris did not. His father, Julius, was a strict disciplinarian. Author Eddie M. Tafoya, who wrote a book titled *Icons of African*

American Comedy, explained that Julius would beat his son at the first sign of trouble. Julius would stress to Chris, "A man doesn't do that."

Chris later learned to appreciate that his dad cared. He often accompanied his father in the newspaper truck through the dark streets of New York in the wee hours of the morning. The elder Rock would relax and talk with his son and the boy's friends. Chris recalled those moments as some of the finest in his life.

Rose cared for her kids—and just about any other child in the neighborhood who needed help. Her home became so crowded that young Chris would sometimes hide in the bathtub just to find some peace and quiet. Rose took in foster children to make extra money and to give children without parents a home. She extended that outlook to her teaching.

"I grew up in a time where teachers weren't really taught to care about kids," Rose explained in a 2008 interview with *MSNBC.com* reporter Danielle Brennan. "Back then black kids were favored if you were light-skinned, had long hair and dressed well. . . . When I became a teacher, I said I was going to like all the dirty children. Every day I made sure to always have a shopping bag with soap and extra clothes so I could catch that kid at the door."

Rose saw the potential in all kids. She equated "greatness" to being a good person. She believed Chris was growing into greatness. Rose also saw fame in his future. She thought her son would become a famous writer.

His parents realized that Chris would struggle to reach his potential attending the poorly funded schools in his neighborhood. So starting in second grade, they had him bused to a school in Bensonhurst, a mostly white neighborhood in Brooklyn.

What Rose and Julius meant as a move to help Chris became one of the worst experiences of his life. Rock was among the first black students at the school. He noticed signs reading "NIGGER, GO HOME" being raised into the air by racist whites.

"I would get beat up every day, called 'nigger' and spit on," Rock told *New York Times* interviewer Cindy Pearlman in 2001. "You get used to it. I couldn't fight back. I was so outnumbered, so I would just stand there and take it. The worst part is that, after a while, your spirit is broken. I'd go to my parents and say, 'Take me out of there.' But they thought it was a better school. I guess it toughened me up."

On the occasions he did fight back, he did so violently. He admitted that he hurt a couple classmates to prove that he could not be pushed around. But he mostly tried to mind his own business and hope he was ignored.

Chris eventually realized that he was a much better joke-teller than he was a fighter. He worked to avoid trouble with his wit. Rather than attempt to intimidate bullies to stay out of a fight, he used his humor to disarm potential attackers.

His frightening experiences at school affected his desire to learn, as he explained to Larry King in 2001. "It wasn't that I was a bad student," he said. "It's just I figured out school at a young age. . . . First of all, if you get an A, they treat you different, but if you get a B, you're in the same class as kids with Fs. So I just knew I wasn't going to get an A, and just why am I going to bust my behind to be with a kid with an F? . . . I can read, I can write, I can count my change."

Chris did not see the point of being a good student. After all, his uneducated father made more money than his educated mother. But he came to understand the value of a strong education. He has refused as an adult to provide money for relatives who planned to use it to launch a career in show business. But he did give them money toward college tuition. He believed that would allow them to use their college knowledge and training if their careers failed in the entertainment world.

When Chris was in school, his home was his sanctuary. He brought over neighborhood friends to meet his family. He was proud of his parents. He never clashed with his father despite the strict discipline. Being the oldest child, he understood the motivation of his dad to keep him moving in a positive direction. He knew that other fathers in the area had abandoned their families, becoming alcoholics or drug addicts. He appreciated his father.

When Chris was a young child, he emulated superhero Spider-Man. He later watched popular TV shows, such as the crime drama *Starsky and Hutch*, with his brother. They pretended to be police officers in Los Angeles just like their fictional heroes. About thirty years later, Rock was offered the part of black informant "Huggy Bear" in a movie remake of the show, but he turned it down. Rock yearned only to play one of the lead roles.

Chris showed an early fascination for comedians. He stayed up late to watch *The Tonight Show* with iconic host Johnny Carson. He studied the stand-up comics who often graced the stage. He was thrilled when legendary black comedian Bill Cosby filled in for Carson as host. Rock has always considered Cosby as the man to which all younger black comedians must be compared.[1]

"I was a really, really hardcore comedy addict," Rock explained to *Life* magazine writer David Bennun. "It was the only thing I liked. It's still the only thing I like. My dad liked being funny, but I broke it down to a science. I realized, girls, if you make them laugh, anything can happen. I never [got a girlfriend] or anything, but the girls that did like me, I made [them] laugh."

Yet success for Chris appeared unlikely. His frightening school experiences soured him on formal education. He dropped out after tenth grade. Chris, however, later used negative experiences in his life, including the bullying he endured, as material for his comedy career.

Though Chris received his general equivalency diploma at age seventeen, he lost his direction. He worked at McDonald's. He helped his father deliver newspapers. He toiled as an orderly at a mental hospital. He cleaned tables at a Red Lobster restaurant. But he never drifted toward a life of crime that often landed other inner city youths in jail.

Rock studied broadcast journalism for one year at a community college and briefly flirted with entering that field. Though a career as a reporter or news anchor never materialized, his interest in current events played a role in the material he later used in his routines on stage.

By his late teenage years, Rock also began listening to musicians that spoke to him. The genres of hip-hop and rap were taking hold on the East Coast. Rock embraced the early hip-hop pioneers, such as Grandmaster Flash, Run DMC, and LL Cool J. They were like poets to him. They expressed feelings that black teenagers could identify.

"[They] were godlike figures to me and still are," Rock told David Keeps of *Best Life* magazine in 2007. "Rap is the first art form created by free black people. Jazz, blues, and [rhythm and blues] were all born during segregation. And before rap, every entertainer put on a suit and cut his hair and tried to be a grown-up. The rappers were really about being 17."

Rock began putting his own ideas on paper. He scribbled down comedy routines, just like his preacher grandfather did with his sermons. Rock began to ask for stage time at New York comedy clubs. He was often turned away. He earned just five dollars for his first gig, at a club called Catch a Rising Star. When he received a chance to perform, he usually earned about seven dollars a night. That was no way to make a living. Audiences often sat stone-faced as Rock attempted in vain to make them laugh.

Frustration set in. He was so angered at being booed off stage that on one occasion he spilled a drink on the head of patron. He was still too young and immature to emotionally handle the criticism that all comedians must endure.

Fate soon stepped in—aided by Rock's growing talent. It was 1986. Rock was preparing to appear at a New York club called The Comic Strip when he spotted superstar comedian and actor Eddie Murphy. Rock was introduced to Murphy, who stuck around to watch his routine. He was brilliant. He impressed Murphy, who asked him to perform a bit part as a parking valet in his upcoming movie, *Beverly Hills Cop II.*

Murphy proved to be the mentor Rock needed. He suggested that Rock study the greats of comedy past and present. Murphy recommended that he learn the nuances of the comedic geniuses, including Bill Cosby and Richard Pryor. Rock did just that. He not only watched the best in the business, but he also noted which jokes drew laughs and which did not.

But tragedy was right around the corner. His father, Julius, died unexpectedly in 1988. His twenty-two-year-old son was devastated. It was a time in Rock's life that he needed his father to guide him. As the oldest child, he was expected to assume leadership of the family. But he was simply not prepared mentally or financially. He was not making enough money to provide significant help.

Rock decided to give his comedy career one more year. His desire to study the stars of stand-up grew in intensity. He listened to the comedic timing of such legends as Woody Allen, Flip Wilson, George Carlin, and Don Rickles. He soaked in how rising superstars, such as Jerry Seinfeld, delivered their punch lines. He was taking his craft more seriously than ever because he understood that he was embarking on a final effort to make a career in comedy work for him.

The hard work paid off. Rock honed his craft well enough to motivate Murphy to invite him to perform on an HBO stand-up special titled *Uptown Comedy Express*. A growing reputation as a dirty comic led to Rock receiving a chance to do a routine a year later in a performance film titled *Comedy's Dirtiest Dozen*. In that routine, which was far from polished, he expressed his anger at the mistrust of many black youth.

"White America is so scared of black teenagers that walk down the street that women are grabbing hold of their mace, everybody's tucking in their chains . . . [and] getting in their karate stances," he began. "I looked up in the air and there's a bunch of old ladies [on] their phones. They're dialing 9-1 . . . and just waiting for them to do something."[2]

Rock drew attention in 1988 with his role in a film aimed at black audiences titled *I'm Gonna Git You Sucka*. His performance led to an appearance on the

Arsenio Hall Show, a talk show hosted by the popular black comedian Arsenio Hall. It was on that program that Rock caught the attention of *Saturday Night Live* executive producer Lorne Michaels. Michaels invited Rock to a casting audition in 1990.

The life and career of Chris Rock was about to take a dramatic turn.

Chapter 3

BIRTH OF A SUPERSTAR

<hr />

Chris Rock was not a confident comedian when his plane landed in Chicago in 1990. He was about to audition for *Saturday Night Live*, the skit TV show that was still blazing new trails in comedy twenty years after its first airing.

And he did not think he was going to be selected. After all, he was competing against great talent, such as Chris Farley, David Spade, and Adam Sandler.

Rock was in his hotel room following the audition when SNL executive producer Lorne Michaels asked Rock to take a limousine ride. They discussed the tradition of the show as they rode around the streets of Chicago. Rock hoped Michaels would invite him to join the cast, but it took quite some time for the words to be uttered.

When Rock finally learned that he had been selected, he was content with his career.

"The day I got on SNL, I was like, 'Okay, even if I play comedy clubs for the rest of my life, it's a pretty great life,'" he told *Best Life* reporter David Keeps.

He proved himself wrong. His experience on *Saturday Night Live* was among the worst of his career. At the age of twenty-four, he was not prepared mentally or emotionally to embrace the work ethic needed to thrive. He was only willing to enjoy the trappings of his newfound fame and fortune. Rock did not take the job seriously enough. He sometimes showed up late to the set for rehearsals after long nights of partying.

Perhaps that was one reason that Rock remained out of the spotlight. It is certain that he played a secondary role to longtime *SNL* standouts such as Phil Hartman, Mike Myers, and David Spade, who had helped the show regain critical acclaim after a down period in the mid-1980s.

Rock was billed as the next Eddie Murphy, who starred on the show a decade earlier. But Rock developed just one memorable character during his three years on *SNL*. That was radical talk-show host Nat X, who sported a brightly colored African shirt and wild afro hairstyle. In one bit, he explored why white athletes dominate the sport of ice hockey.

"I was watchin' a hockey game and I noticed there were no black people," Nat X said with angry look on his face. "So I looked into this example of the white man once again keepin' the black man down and found out why there were no black people in hockey. . . . No [black man] is going to go anywhere [where] there is a bunch of crazy white people wearin' masks and carryin' sticks!"

Rock later admitted that he gave in to the pressure of performing on the legendary show. He was simply too immature as a person to deal with comparisons to past *SNL* greats, such as John Belushi, Dan Aykroyd, and Murphy, and it wore on him. But Rock did develop positive relationships that would later benefit his career. He established a friendship with fellow *SNL* cast member Adam Sandler that would lead to the pair teaming up in successful comedy films well after both had left the show.

Rock achieved more in movies than he did on *Saturday Night Live* during that time. He received praise for his performance as a drug addict in the 1991 film *New Jack City*. He played a supporting role in a Murphy film titled *Boomerang*. He also released his first comedy album, *Born Suspect*.

Frustration over his role in *SNL* motivated Rock to quit the show in 1993, before his contract ran out. He joined the popular sitcom *In Living Color* just as it was ending its run. He starred in and helped write *CB4*, a comedy film about a rap group. But none gained critical acclaim, and he had no steady work. His career was at a standstill.

"I didn't have no house, I felt like I had squandered my life," he told Keeps. "I'd made some money, but I kind of felt like, that what the [heck] have you been doing?"

He later admitted that *CB4* could have been a far better movie if he had been more mature at the time. He simply did not put in the effort to make it the best it could be. The film revolved around Rock's character, Albert, a nice kid who acted like a gangster so he could boost the fortunes of his rap band. Rock also created Albert's father in the film to be the spitting image of his late father, Julius.

Rock eventually grasped that he would never realize his potential if his work ethic did not improve. He soon decided to return to what he did best— stand-up comedy. He kept up with current events in the news and pop culture. He scribbled down ideas for routines, just as he had done as a novice comedian.

But he was no longer a novice comedian. When he returned to the stage, he had grown far more polished and confident.

Earlier in his career, he would open his show by asking the audience how they were doing. He now began his act immediately. He had once looked uncomfortable in front of a crowd, but now he was self-assured. He once left the stage to silence, head down, angry and frustrated—he now walked off to laughter with his head held high.

The new, improved Chris Rock landed a 1994 HBO special titled *Big Ass Jokes*. His thirty-minute routine in front of a huge applauding crowd in Atlanta did little for his career, but it proved he had grown as a comedian. Rock showed versatility in his material. He made his audience laugh with more than just racial humor. He mixed in jokes about the differences in the two genders.

"I like women. My mother's a woman—that helps," he began. "Women control the whole thing. . . . Women have male friends, platonic friends. What is that [all] about? That's like the biggest scam in the world. No man ever looked at a woman and said '[darn] she's [beautiful], she is so [beautiful]. She's *so* [beautiful] I want to make her my friend.'"

Despite his growth as a stand-up comic, his career remained stagnant. Rock recorded *Big Ass Jokes* in front of a mostly black audience. He had yet to break through to white America. The TV roles he landed reflected that. He appeared in sitcoms such as *Martin* and *The Fresh Prince of Bel-Air*, both of which featured black casts.

All people, blacks and whites, had embraced black comics, such as Bill Cosby and Eddie Murphy. Rock knew he could not maximize his star potential without attracting the same fan base. But he did not want to compromise his talent and passion for embracing social and political issues simply to gain greater fame and fortune.

The three years after Rock left *Saturday Night Live* were the toughest of his career. Rock never gave up, but he no longer thought about being a star. He was simply motivated to make enough money to pay his bills. He was not depressed, but he felt his chance at greatness had come and gone.

Just as Rock hit bottom, he skyrocketed to the top. In 1996, cable network HBO saw enough potential in Rock to give him an hour-long special titled *Bring the Pain*, which was taped at the Takoma Theater in Washington, D.C. Rock exploded onto the national scene. His confidence on stage, as well as his improved delivery and timing, was never more evident. His ability to create humor from even the most disturbing news events of the time caused both laughter and criticism that led to publicity.

Rock wasted no time taking controversial stands. He opened the show by ridiculing Washington mayor Marion Barry in his own city. Rock offered that Barry had no business participating in the recent Million Man March, a huge show of solidarity among African-American men throughout America. Rock claimed that Barry was not a positive role model after being caught with crack cocaine and spending six months in prison. He then chided those who voted Barry back into office.

"Marion Barry at the Million Man March," Rock began. "How'd he get a ticket? It was a day of *positivity*. How'd he get in, man? Marion Barry at the Million Man March. You know what that means? Even in our finest hour, we had a crackhead on stage." A few boos broke through the laughter. "Boo if you want," Rock replied. "You know I'm right."

Rock was just starting to roll.

"How in the [heck] did Marion Barry get his job back? Smoked crack, got his job back. . . . If you get caught smoking crack at McDonald's, you can't get your job back. . . . They're not going to trust you around the Happy Meals! Who ran against him? Who was so bad that they lost to a crackhead?"

Rock later embarked on the most famous part of his routine—and one of the most controversial comedic bits in American history. His "Black People vs. Niggas" rant prompted both high praise and sharp criticism. He yearned to draw a distinction between the hardworking, law-abiding African Americans and those that he believed were not embracing their responsibilities.

Critics claimed that it was self-defeating for African Americans to use a derogatory word like "niggas"—a racist word that angered black people if whites directed it at them. Critics further contended that the social and economic hardships of surviving in the inner city play a huge role in the negative behavior of some black people—in this case, those Rock criticized as "niggas." He was oversimplifying a complex and deeply rooted societal problem for laughs. Others, however, argued in favor of Rock, claiming that poverty is no excuse for any behavior that casts a negative light on other African Americans and their community.

Despite the controversy, *Bring the Pain* took America by storm. *Variety*, a publication that reviews various forms of entertainment throughout the country, praised the HBO special as "one of the truly remarkable hours of comedy ever to air on television."

Rock's message in *Bring the Pain* had reached beyond the United States. Leo Benedictus, a critic from the London newspaper the *Guardian,* praised Rock for having the courage to hold some of his fellow black people accountable for their actions. Benedictus wrote: "By venting his disgust for such behavior—along with his disgust for domestic violence . . . drug addiction and other urban ills—he became a hero for making something inspirational out of simple decency. . . . Equality, decency, education, restraint: over and over, these are what Rock pleads for, with a vigor and a choice of words that makes these . . . topics actually funny."

The success of *Bring the Pain* solidified Rock as a giant of modern stand-up comedy. What was more important to him was that it justified his career path. He entered the project feeling that it might be his last chance to prove himself as a comedian.

Despite his time on *Saturday Night Live* and his previous shows on HBO, he felt that his career was on the brink of extinction in the mid-1990s. He focused on becoming the best he could be on stage. And all his hard work had paid off.

Rock won two coveted Emmy Awards for *Bring the Pain.* It won honors in both the "Outstanding Variety, Music or Comedy Special" and "Outstanding Writing for a Variety or Music Program" categories.

It also earned a Certificate of Merit from the San Francisco International Film Festival.

Rock actually competed against himself for the Emmy Award for writing. He had also received a nomination as a correspondent for the comedy show *Politically Incorrect With Bill Maher* at the 1996 Democratic and Republican national conventions.

Suddenly, he was everywhere. He served as a spokesperson for shoe manufacturer Nike. He made his first appearance on *The Tonight Show*, fulfilling a lifelong dream. World famous director Steven Spielberg asked him to create a series of comedy videos. And in 1997, he signed a deal with HBO to host his own talk show titled, the *Chris Rock Show*.

Rock strived to make his program as hard-hitting as his stage act. He not only performed stand-up routines, but he also acted out skits and invited controversial guests to interview. The show allowed Rock to speak to both black and white audiences. He expressed his feelings about politics and pop culture, which angered some guests. Actress and comedian Whoopi Goldberg scolded him on the air for what she perceived as Rock berating celebrities.

However, the critics approved. *Entertainment Weekly* writer Ken Tucker praised Rock for rejecting the motivation of many modern-day performers, particularly musicians, that he claimed catered only to the African-American community.

"Rock wants to . . . speak for and to everyone," he wrote. "Such an ambition may account for his material's [disorganized] quality—Rock hits higher highs and lower lows than any comedian around. But when a joke or sketch flops, the energy and ideas [supporting] his material keep the show strong and funny."

Soon, Rock explored additional outlets for his talents. While the *Chris Rock Show* was gaining popularity, he was compiling bits from his funniest routines for a book titled *Rock This!* Rock dedicated the book to his father, "the funniest guy I've ever known."

The book featured a myriad of Rock bits and topics, including racism, marriage, politics, religion, relationships, drugs, and love. He also related humorous personal stories about his childhood and beyond.

Among the funniest was his chance meeting with a former classmate at the predominantly white school he attended in his youth. Rock explained that the man who happened to be his limousine driver on a trip to Los Angeles used to spit in his face. Rock briefly felt the same fear he experienced when he used to encounter the same man as a teenager in school:

Fear is the same whether you're 7 years old or 30. But he talked like we were best friends. He said he told everybody he went to school with me, but nobody believed him.

Meanwhile, I'm thinking, "Why don't you show them the eye you kicked out of my head?"

I was uncomfortable the whole ride.

When we got back to my house I made sure to give him a big tip. I knew it would mess with his mind.

Why? On "Bugs Bunny," when would Elmer Fudd get the maddest? When Bugs shot him in the head? No. When Bugs dropped an anvil on his head? No. It was when Bugs kissed him. So my tip was like a kiss. I also figured that if I didn't give him a big tip, that in his mind it would validate all the time he kicked my [butt].[1]

Rock was on top of the world. In 1998, his *Roll With the New* won a Grammy Award for Best Spoken Comedy Album. A year later, the *Chris Rock Show* captured an Emmy for Outstanding Writing for a Variety or Music Program.

Rock was soaring to the top of the world professionally. But he was also seeking to become more fulfilled as a person. There had been something missing in his life for quite some time. It was love. He recognized that he wanted to find his soul mate. And soon thereafter, he yearned to be a father. All those dreams, too, were about to be realized.

Chapter 4

NEW WIFE, NEW LIFE

Chris Rock was bored. He was unsatisfied with his life. He did not fully realize it until one fateful afternoon.

One day, he was hanging with friends at the mall after watching a matinee at the theater. Suddenly, it struck him. There was something missing, as he explained to *Best Life* magazine interviewer David Keeps.

"You know, guys," he said. "It is really depressing that it is three o'clock and none of us has to pick up our kids. This is just sad!"

Since 1993, Rock had been dating Malaak Compton, a publicist for the United Nations Children's Fund (UNICEF). However, his lifestyle had not changed. His career was thriving. He did not know why he was unhappy—until that moment.

In the *Best Life* interview, Rock said:

> It had nothing to do with my career. It was all about what I'd done in my personal life. I was in my thirties, but I caught myself doing the same stuff I was doing when I was 24. I used to wake up every day at either 11 o'clock or the first phone call, whichever came first! And 11 would turn into 12 or one. I was working at nightclubs, so I guess I had a reason to be out all the time, but I remember thinking, "My God, why are you doing this?"

> You get tired of dating, you get tired of looking. You just get physically tired. And you get to a point where you realize that the problems you are going to have with one person, you are probably going to have with another. There are certain issues in your life that are always going to come up, so you might as well just stop right now and just deal with them with one person.

That one person was Compton, whom he married on November 23, 1996. Rock admitted that the early days of marriage were tough. He found it difficult to have control of his career and dominate his audiences on stage and then return home to an equal relationship.

Rock also had trust issues, though not with his wife. He realized that fame and fortune attracted people who claimed to be his friends but had other motives. He concluded that his only true friends were those who were close to him when he was broke. Those are the only ones he trusts.

While he embraced a more quiet life at home, he explored new roads in his career path. The success from *Bring the Pain* and the *Chris Rock Show* opened up avenues in many different directions, including those on the big screen. He appeared with stars Mel Gibson and Danny Glover as a detective in the blockbuster action film, *Lethal Weapon 4*. He provided the voice of a guinea pig in the Eddie Murphy movie, *Dr. Doolittle*.

The most interesting was yet to come. Rock was cast as Rufus, the thirteenth apostle of Jesus, in a star-studded 1999 comedy titled *Dogma*. The plot revolves around two angels banished by God who wish to return to His good graces. They do not realize that if they got back to heaven, they will have proved that

God can make mistakes and is therefore not unfailing. That places the existence of the universe in peril.

God sends a helper to convince an earthly woman to thwart the angels' plans. Rufus is a dead man who falls from the sky while the woman and two of her helpers are walking down the highway. Rock tells her that he has come down to earth to help her change the Bible because there is no mention of him as the thirteenth apostle. He claims he was edited out of the holy book because he is black.

"Jesus wasn't white," Rufus says. "Jesus was black. . . . White folks only want to hear the good [stuff]: life eternal, a place in God's Heaven. But as soon as you hear that they're getting this good [stuff] from a black Jesus, you freak. And that, my friends, is called hypocrisy. A black man can steal your stereo, but he can't be your savior."

Despite his ventures into film, Rock was still a stand-up comedian at heart. He had simply hoped that *Bring the Pain* would be better than his previous HBO specials featuring his live act. He figured on reaping small rewards if it was successful. He anticipated an offer to do a sitcom if he was lucky enough.

So when his performance in *Bring the Pain* resulted in national attention, Rock was shocked. He could not believe the controversial routines were being debated on sophisticated news networks, such as C-SPAN. He started to become uncomfortable with his popularity. He did not want to compromise his material to suit it to wide audiences.

So rather than tape his next special from a venue such as Radio City Music Hall in New York, he scheduled it for the famed Apollo Theater in Harlem, where he could perform for a mostly black crowd. He believed that anything associated with black audiences is considered by many to be a small event because it likely did not receive attention outside the black community. He wanted to show that it could be a major event, so he called it *Bigger and Blacker*.

Rock made every subject fair game in the city in which he was raised. He was louder and angrier than ever. He lost none of the profanity that laced his performance in *Bring the Pain*. He embarked on a rant against every perceived social ill in America, including racism, youth violence, AIDS, and gun control.

Among the funniest bits was about those who grumble that their race has it the toughest in the United States. Rock claimed that no group has it harder than American Indians. The plight of the American Indian has indeed been tragic, but once again, Rock was able to raise awareness of a serious situation through humor. He sought to focus on the mistreatment of the Indian population that began when white populations arrived on the North American shores and continued until they had been killed through war or disease or had lost their freedom through forced placement on reservations. The American Indian remains the most economically depressed minority group in the country.

As the crowd clapped its approval, Rock barked:

So everybody [complains] about how bad their people got it—nobody got it worse than the American Indian. Everybody need to calm the [heck] down. Indians got it bad. Indians got it the worst. You know how bad the Indians got it? When's the last time you met two Indians? You ain't never met two Indians.

I have seen a polar bear ride a . . . tricycle in my lifetime. I have never seen an Indian family that's chilling out at Red Lobster. Never seen it. Everybody wants to save the environment. I see trees every day. I don't never see no Indians. I went to the Macy's Thanksgiving Day Parade this year. They didn't have enough Indians. They had a bunch of Pilgrims. When it came time for the Indians, they had had three real Indians . . . and the rest was a bunch of Puerto Ricans with feathers in their hair. . . . That's not Pocahontas. That's Jennifer Lopez!"[1]

Those in attendance roared with laughter. *Bigger and Blacker* earned the 1999 Grammy award for Best Spoken Comedy Album. *Variety* critic Ray Richmond, who watched Rock rant at the Apollo Theater, praised him for not swearing just for effect. He thought some of the routine could be considered in bad taste, but he enjoyed Rock's honesty and willingness to continue taking chances in his comedy.

"The act is laced with at least as much profanity as is typical for Rock, though coming from his intelligent perch it rarely feels [unjustified]," Richmond wrote. "If you like your comedy to be breathtakingly brash and candid, Rock remains the gold standard for the new millennium."

The new millennium had something else in store for Rock and America. On September 11, 2001, the terrorist attacks on New York and Washington, D.C., proved traumatic for the nation. It was as disturbing as any single event since the Japanese bombing of Pearl Harbor sixty years earlier that launched U.S. involvement in World War II. And it had a strong effect on Rock. He lent his time and name to a telethon that aired ten days later in which he spoke about the heroism of a single New York firefighter named Tim Brown, who was still digging through the rubble on the World Trade Center site to find more evidence of victims of the tragedy.

The destruction got Rock thinking about what was missing in his life. He had been married for five years without planning anything for their future. In the midst of all the chaos, he and Malaak decided to have children.

Rock took a philosophical approach to his impending fatherhood after his wife got pregnant. He told talk-show host Oprah Winfrey that he preferred to have a daughter because he thought he would be too hard on a boy (the couple eventually had two girls). He said he appreciated that babies do not care if their parents are rich or poor. They are happy to be loved.

He knew exactly what kind of father he would be. Rock was looking forward to spending time with his child. He wanted to have energy and health so he could play with and teach his kid. He yearned to forge a friendship with his children. As he spoke, Winfrey recognized just from seeing his face that he was looking forward to fatherhood. She exclaimed that she was thrilled to learn about a black child coming into the world with willing and able parents.

"When you first told me about the baby, I could sense your joy and excitement," she said. "I'm always happy to see that in black parents because so many of our children came into the world with no one anticipating our arrival."

Rock's lifestyle had already changed by that time. He no longer hung out with his friends at night. When he was not working, he was at home with his wife. He was expanding horizons in his personal life. He was exploring his interests in art and music.

He had always felt a sense of pride about being black, but he began rooting for other blacks to succeed. Rock recalled that there were no blacks on television when he was a child. He found himself grinning one day when he noticed that a number of reporters on an HBO sports program he was watching were black. He hoped that race was never an issue in the lives of his children.

Rock revealed in the 2002 Oprah interview that he believed his career was like a great unknown. He had been asked to star in sitcoms, which could have been profitable. But he did not feel sitcoms best suited his style and interests as a comedian. He missed performing on the *Chris Rock Show*, which had ended two years earlier. He missed informing people about the news and pop culture in a humorous way.

By that time, Rock was ready to roll. He had taken himself out of the public spotlight from 1998 to 2000 because he had grown tired of watching or listening to himself perform and he feared he was going to be burned out.

Rock worked behind the scenes on several projects. He served as executive producer of the TV sitcom *The Hughleys*, which premiered in September 1998 and ran for four seasons. The show featured a successful black vending-machine salesman who moves his family from a Los Angeles ghetto to an all-white neighborhood in San Francisco. The family works to adjust to their new lifestyle while being true to their roots.

The Hughleys placed Rock squarely in the mainstream. It aired on ABC for two seasons before it was picked up by cable network UPN. The ratings began strong before tailing off. Though many critics panned the show, including *Variety* reviewer Ray Richmond, who claimed that its humor focused too intently on racism, it earned a number of individual and overall honors. It won the Young Artist Award for Best TV Comedy Series in 1999. It was nominated for a 2000 American Cinema Foundation award in the sitcom category. A year later, *The Hughleys* captured a Prism Award for Outstanding Comedy Series.

Rock also yearned to maximize his potential in films. He cowrote and starred in the 2001 comedy *Down to Earth*, which was a remake of a popular 1978 movie titled *Heaven Can Wait*. Rock could identify with comic Lance Barton, his character in the movie who was shown bombing on stage as the film began.

Two women sitting in the balcony wanted him to hear their boos so badly that they were gargling to clear their throats.

Barton was not discouraged by the reaction to his performance. But as he was biking home, he was run over by a truck and killed. He is next seen in heaven, where it is determined that it was not yet his time to die. His soul was allowed to return to earth in the body of a filthy rich white man named Charles Wellington. Wellington is married to a woman who hates him.

Rock's character soon falls in love with a good-hearted black woman who is trying to help sick children with no health insurance get treated in a hospital that Wellington's corporation owns. The soulful Barton's voice and words coming out in the soulless body of a fifty-year-old white man sparks the funniest moments in the film.

Critics, however, slammed the movie. They embraced the Chris Rock who took chances and tackled serious issues as a stage comedian. They understood that he used profanity and crude subject matter to create laughter. They would have preferred to see that formula of success translated onto the big screen.

"When he's doing stand-up (his own, not the intentionally awful kind delivered by Lance), Rock's satire can be startling," wrote *CNN.com* reviewer Paul Tatara. "Here, he just marches out one tired situation after another in which an older white man makes people uncomfortable by acting like a young black man. . . . There's no escaping the fact that this is a terrible picture, even if you're not expecting much. The best move at this point would be for Rock to reconvene his TV crew and start making vicious fun of himself."

New York Times reviewer Elvis Mitchell offered that Rock was gaining confidence as an actor, but still needed to grow. And he agreed with others that Rock was not being true to the style that made him a sensation on stage.

"Because of his fan base and its expectations, '*Down to Earth*' seems to be skimming the surface," Mitchell wrote. "Mr. Rock's fans, who'll recognize some of his stand-up jokes in Lance's routines, are going to want a movie with the same [hard-hitting] funkiness that he brings to his stand-up, and they won't find that."

The funkiness Mitchell believed was missing did appear in *Pootie Tang*, another film Rock produced and starred in that year. Pootie Tang was a character taken from the *Chris Rock Show*. He was a ladies' man, recording artist, and actor who was beloved by children and hated by the evil Lecter Corporation, which sold cigarettes and alcohol to kids. His strength comes from a belt bestowed upon him by his father, who was one of the many characters in the movie played by Rock.

Black audiences and some younger white moviegoers embraced *Pootie Tang*. Rock later claimed he was proud of the film, but the mainstream media blasted it. Among those who panned it was arguably the most respected film critic in the country, Roger Ebert, who believed the funny moments were few in a movie that he called "disorganized, senseless and chaotic."

Rock was still trying to find himself as an actor. He hoped someday to work with the modern greats of American film. He began thinking about directing movies. But by 2002, he had other matters on his mind. He was about to become a father.

Chapter 5

FATHERHOOD AND NEW WORK

It was June 28, 2002, when his wife, Malaak, gave birth to daughter Lola Simone. And from that moment forward, Chris Rock dedicated himself to being the finest father he could be.

It was not difficult for Rock. He scoffs at those who complain that they must sacrifice to raise their kids. He has relished the job ever since he set eyes on the new member of his family. It also brought back memories of his father and childhood.

He recalled asking himself if his dad was content raising him. Rock wondered if his father would be having more fun if he did not have to spend so much time with his kids. Rock understood from the moment he became a father that his thinking was all wrong. He learned that fun and fatherhood go hand in hand.

Speaking with National Public Radio interviewer Leke Sanusi in August 2012, well after second daughter, Zahra, was born, Rock said:

> I'm fortunate. . . . I grew up, two parents, my dad was really into it, so just by osmosis, I'm just really into it. I never really looked at it as a chore or whatever. When I hear people talk about juggling, or the sacrifices they make for their children, I look at them like they're crazy, because "sacrifice" infers that there was something better to do than being with your children.

> And I've never been with my kids and gone, "Man, I wish I was on my stage right now." I've never been with my kids and gone, "Man, it'd be so great if I was on a movie set right now." But I've been doing a movie and wished that I was with my kids, I've been on tour and wished that I was with my kids. Being with my kids is the

best, most fun thing, it's a privilege. It's not something I call a sacrifice.

Rock even relished the dirtiest of jobs, such as changing diapers. It brought him closer to Lola and made him realize that caring *for* her showed how much he cared *about* her. His life and career became tied to his children.

On one occasion, asthmatic daughter Zahra spent a night in the hospital. Rock never realized how frightened he could be. He realized that he would give his life to save hers. He watched his kids grow smarter and prettier, and he realized they brought great joy into his life.

But with joy brought professional responsibility. He became more motivated than ever in his career because he yearned to take care of his children emotionally and financially. He felt that he had to maximize his talent so he could provide for Lola and Zahra.

"You don't know how good you can be at anything until you have kids," he told *Best Life* magazine reporter David Keeps. "My single friends, the three or four I have, they're always like, 'I don't have enough money.' I'm like, 'Hey have some kids, you'll make money.' There is something about kids that makes you make it happen. . . . There is no relaxing when you have kids."

The responsibility he felt went beyond reading bedtime stories and ensuring their financial well-being. He wanted to raise them to boast strong morals and values. He understood the importance of fostering a positive self-image. He was a wealthy man, but he did not want his daughters to respect money over intelligence. He thought it was sad that a country that once revered a genius, such as Albert Einstein, now took more interest in the life stories of billionaires.

Rock also understood that some women define themselves by the men in their lives. He hoped that Lola and Zahra found love, but he also strived to make them emotionally strong and self-sufficient. He introduced them to such impressive role models as Oprah Winfrey and helped teach them about the world.

But as much as he enjoyed spending time with his daughters, Rock took after his father in his stress of discipline. He believed that cracking down on bad behavior is not a sign of anger. It was simply tough love meant to make them better people.

"This whole notion that kids are nice is just [wrong], because they need to be socialized and they need to be shown boundaries," he told Keeps. "You have to teach kids to love. They're hatin' when they come out. They're hittin' and saying mean things I never have to tell my daughters, 'Hey! Stop sayin' nice things! How dare you kiss your sister like that!' Kids are born hating, and your love teaches them to love."

Meanwhile, Rock was learning a few things about films. Many of those in which he acted before the birth of his first daughter were aimed strictly at inner-city black audiences. The same could not be said about the 2002 action comedy *Bad Company*, in which he played the twin brother of a dead spy. Most reviews criticized the performance of Rock, the script, or both. They believed him to be stiff and unnatural as an actor.

But Rock refused to accept defeat in the world of film. And in 2003, he showed his talent and versatility in a comedy titled *Head of State*. Rock starred and cowrote the script in which he played an obscure politician named Mays Gilliam, who was chosen to run for president of the United States. He also realized a professional dream by directing the movie.

Unlike previous Rock comedies, which were not true to his style of lampooning serious issues, *Head of State* serves to criticize the election process in America. In the film, Democrats chose his character to lose the election, but also to gain black votes for the next election. When he learns of the plot, he becomes determined to win.

The climax of the film is his fiery speech at a campaign rally. He turns off the teleprompter, thereby dismissing his prepared speech, and speaks from the heart. Rock displays his growing acting talent as he stirs up the crowd.

"How many of you have children that they call stupid?" he asks the crowd. "Don't be ashamed. It ain't your fault. I asked my niece the other day, 'What's four plus four?' She said, 'Forty-four.' But that ain't her fault. That's the school's fault. If your child's school has [old] books and brand-new metal detectors, let me hear you say, 'That ain't right!'"

The crowd screamed out, "That ain't right!"

"How many of you live in a city you can't afford to live in? That ain't right!" he continued. "How many of you work in a mall you can't afford to shop in? That ain't right! . . . We got nurses who work in hospitals they can't even afford to get sick in. That ain't right! It isn't right. [It's] dead wrong. I'm Mays Gilliam, and I'm running for President of the United States of America."

Rock was improving as an actor. And that was recognized by critics. He even received a positive review from none other than Roger Ebert, who had slammed *Pootie Tang* a year earlier.

"What Rock brings to [the film] is brashness—zingers that hurt," Ebert wrote. "'What kind of a drug policy,' he wants to know, 'makes crack [cocaine] cheaper than asthma medicine?'" Ebert even expressed his belief that Rock was an ideal candidate to host the Academy Awards, which he did two years later.

His stock as an actor and writer was rising. But Rock always knew that his greatest talent was as a stand-up comedian. He understood that he had most control over his material and performance on stage. It was all a solo effort. So in 2004, he returned to his comedic roots with another HBO special titled *Never Scared*.

The show was taped during his performances at the DAR Convention Hall in Washington, D.C., and he turned it into an album. It featured Rock doing what he does best—taking serious topics and transforming them into humor. He had new experiences in his personal life to use as material, including fatherhood.

Rock, however, focused more on politics and pop culture. He joked about music star Michael Jackson, marriage, affirmative action, illegal drugs, terrorism, the war in Iraq, and the grave topic of world hunger. He even entertained the audience with a short routine about his love for doughnuts.

The formula that transformed Rock from a failing comedian into perhaps the best in America was still working. Rock studied current events and pop culture. He focused on experiences in his personal life, which could be used to make people laugh. He had become a prepared professional. He had matured, and he understood that he had others in his life to care for. The well-being of his daughters had become a driving force.

So were his political beliefs. He attacked one of his favorite subjects in one of the longer bits in *Never Scared*—President George W. Bush. Rock spoke about mediocrity in lampooning the most powerful leader in the free world.

"That's all America is—a nation in the middle," he said as he paced the stage. "A nation of B and C students. Well, let's keep it real, OK? A black C student can't run no company. A black C student can't even be the manager of Burger King. Meanwhile, a white C student just happens to be the president of the United States of America!"

Never Scared was nominated for Emmy Awards for Best Writing and Best Variety, Music or Comedy Show. The album captured a Grammy Award for Best Comedy Album. His success in that endeavor earned him the opportunity to host the prestigious Academy Awards in February 2005. Only the premier entertainers in the world receive an opportunity to host what is also known as the Oscars. Among them have been talk-show legend Johnny Carson and comedians such as Steve Martin and Billy Crystal.

But Rock never shied away from controversy. After being tabbed to headline the show, he condemned it. He claimed that awards shows in general were "idiotic." He said he rarely watched the Academy Awards. He called it "a fashion show." He criticized the Oscars for failing to award comedy films. He blasted the Academy Awards for what he perceived as failing to nominate African-American actors.

Some laughed off his comments. Others claimed Rock was merely trying to stir up controversy to increase ratings for the show. But many others lambasted him. Among them was Matt Drudge, a talk-show host and creator of an Internet news organization called the *Drudge Report*. Drudge blasted Rock and claimed that many believed he should be removed as Oscar host.

"There is a split out there," Drudge said. "Many of the old timers don't think this is the route to go. Don't go down in the gutter. Don't go foul mouth, potty mouth. Go to celebration of the arts. Go to celebration of humanity. Don't go to this trash talking and don't go into this. What Chris Rock does, is just burn everybody. It's a very curious choice."

Oscar producer Gil Cates felt differently. He backed Rock and added he was looking forward to a funny evening. And he got one. Rock had the Academy Awards audience rolling with his routine about childhood memories of movies and how his views had changed.

"Remember when you were a kid and every movie was incredible?" he asked the celebrity-filled audience. "Every movie was magic. They were all great. Then you grow up and you watch some of those same movies. You're like, 'Rocky V *sucks.*'"

Rock then entertained the crowd with his feelings about what makes the Academy Awards unique. In the process, he might have soothed hard feelings over his earlier criticisms.

"I love the Oscars," he said. "You know why I love the Oscars? Because the Oscars are the only awards show where the people getting awards don't perform. That's right. There's no acting at the Oscars. None at all.

"You go to the Grammys, they're singing. You go to the Tony Awards, they're singing and dancing. . . . But there's no acting at the Oscars at all. Can I get a little acting? Just a 'to be or not to be' or [actor] Morgan Freeman doing a shampoo commercial. Something! The only acting you see at the Oscars is when people act like they're not mad they lost."

Rock was still striving to maximize his own acting talent. However, only his voice was used in the 2005 Disney animated hit *Madagascar*, in which he played Marty the Zebra. Rock also appeared with *Saturday*

Night Live friend Adam Sandler in the remake of a movie about a football team in prison titled *The Longest Yard.*

Rock had gained success as a stand-up comic and comedic film actor. He had been fielding offers to perform in sitcoms, but none suited him. That is, until 2005, when Rock took matters into his own hands. He created, wrote, produced, and narrated a show titled *Everybody Hates Chris.*

The new endeavor brought him back in touch with his experiences as a youth. And it allowed a new generation of fans to learn about a childhood that had affected Rock to that day.

Chapter 6

LOVING *EVERYBODY HATES CHRIS*

The portrayal of black families on television has been criticized for many years.

Until well past the civil rights movement of the late 1950s and 1960s, few African Americans earned roles as regular characters on TV programs. Such was certainly the case with sitcoms.

That began to change in the 1970s. Several shows featuring black families were created during that time, including *The Jeffersons* and *Sanford and Son*. These two shows had great success, but many considered them to be negative representations of black people. The main male characters in the shows were sometimes deceitful, stupid, or both.

An effort was made in the 1980s to present more positive black images. The most notable example was *The Cosby Show*, starring iconic comedian and Rock hero Bill Cosby. His character upheld impeccable moral standards, unlike many of the sitcom African Americans that preceded him. But some felt that program was equally unrealistic. Cosby played a doctor married to a black lawyer. Unlike most African Americans and most Americans in general, they lived a comparatively wealthy lifestyle.

Rock yearned to write and produce a realistic show about a black family, so he beckoned his upbringing in creating *Everybody Hates Chris*. He recalled his hardworking father and loving mother trying to raise a family through financial hardship. He focused on thirteen-year-old Chris Rock growing up in the tough Bedford-Stuyvesant section of New York City. It chronicled his emotional pain as he worked to survive the prejudice and racial taunts at a mostly white school.

The show was a critical success. Rock narrated the new and exciting family sitcom, a TV genre critics complained had grown stale. *Everybody Hates Chris* not only revolved around a young teenager, but it delved into issues, such as marriage, racial tensions, and sibling relationships.

The first show takes place in 1982. Rock's character has the most difficult role in the family as the oldest child. His brother is more confident. His sister receives most of the attention from their parents. His father works two jobs and is aware of every cent spent by his family. His mother sometimes works as well so bills can be paid.

The Chris character not only must play the father figure when both parents are out, but he is the only sibling to be bused to school. He must take several buses to reach Corleone Junior High (a fictional institution named humorously after an Italian mobster), where he is bullied unmercifully as one of the few black students. But he learns that he can use his charm and sense of humor to make new friends.

Everybody Hates Chris sprinkled serious subject matter in with large doses of funny flashbacks. In one episode, Chris allows someone to ride his bicycle, and it is stolen. Chris is out looking for the bike while his family is eating dinner. His sister asks his mother where he is.

"Somebody stole his bike after I told him not to let anybody ride it," she said. "So I smacked him into next week. He'll be back on Tuesday."

The realism in the portrayal of a black family Rock created with the help of his childhood memories brought honors and positive reviews. The show won the 2006 Image Award for Outstanding Comedy Series from the National Association for the Advancement of Colored People (NAACP). It also earned a Golden Globe nomination for Best Series that same year.

Critics were equally kind. *New York Times* reviewer Allesandra Stanley appreciated the humor that was far cleaner than in Rock's stand-up routines. She compared *Everybody Hates Chris* to *The Cosby Show* because of the respect the children in both families showed to their parents.

"Most comedies about the collision of parents and children are set in cozy middle-class America, where the adults are . . . at war with children who roll their eyes, talk back and fearlessly mock their parents' values," Stanley wrote in September 2005. "*Everybody Hates Chris* is the first show in a long time centered on a teenager whose main problem is not adolescent [anxiety], but real life. And Mr. Rock makes it funny, not [depressing] or mean."

The show remained near and dear to Rock's heart. His difficult childhood has stayed with him as an adult. His wealth and fame, as well as his work in show business, keep him close to those who are also rich and renowned. But he feels a kinship for people still struggling in life. He understands that those raised in inner cities as he was have much to overcome and that many of them must fight just to survive.

Some celebrities take for granted the attention they receive from others. Rock especially appreciates those who loved him and cared about him when he was a child or a failing comedian early in his career. He enjoys helping young, struggling comedians, because he remembers how established stars helped him when he was young.

Rock even goes out of his way to say a kind word to people he never met. His attitude is a reflection of his overall cynical view of society. He does not believe most people are willing to treat others kindly. He feels they are mostly out for themselves. It is a philosophy that has strengthened through the years.

"It's not hard to feel hopeless," he said. "My glass is not only half empty, there's a hole in the bottom. But it'll be all right. I always expect people to treat you [terribly]. . . . I'm a barbershop politician. I write jokes for the guy who is earning $700 a week. I try to perk up strangers every day, because I know when I talk to certain people, it means more than it should. It costs me nothing, so yeah, I try to lift spirits as much as I can."[1]

Even when Rock is in the company of greatness, he is never far from his childhood in his mind. He spent Christmas in 2005 at the home of South African leader and Nobel Peace Prize winner Nelson Mandela. He was thousands of miles from New York, yet his thoughts drifted back to sitting on the stoop of his home as a kid. He reflected on how far he had come in life.

He had come quite far—and he continued to explore a wide variety of work opportunities. In 2007, he cowrote and directed a film titled *I Think I Love My Wife*. He took the project more seriously than he had any other movie. He worked with an acting coach and cast dramatic actors rather than comedic actors.

The setting for the movie was suburban New York City. Rock played a successful investment banker with a beautiful wife who is disinterested in sex. His character flirts with other women. But he is not tempted to act upon his fantasies until a beautiful woman from his past reenters his life. His temptation grows when she makes it obvious that she is interested in having an affair.

The project was a departure for Rock. Though there was humor in the movie, it was mostly serious. He was forced to play a character in emotional pain. The character was tortured by what he perceived as a choice between two terrible options—abstaining from marital relations with his wife or cheating on her.

I Think I Love My Wife proved a success at the box office. It was among the most watched movies in America the first week it arrived at the theaters, and it eventually earned $13 million worldwide. But critics offered the same complaint they had about earlier Rock works. They railed against its profanity and offered that it was simply too raunchy.

Entertainment Weekly reviewer Lisa Schwarzbaum enjoyed the more reflective moments of the film. She praised the scenes in which the Rock character spoke about the difficulties of being an upper-middle-class black man in a white world. But she added her belief that Rock still needed to grow as an actor.

"Rock isn't yet a natural actor—he uses the same pursed facial expressions to convey lust, fear, guilt, and dismay at being served chicken by his wife one too many times," she wrote. "And in directing his second feature . . . he can't yet translate his skills as a brilliant comedian into equally sharp focus; his cinematic skills are only mild."

His skills as a stand-up comedian, however, were as strong as ever. Rock filmed stand-up performances in South Africa, England, and the Apollo Theater in New York for his special titled *Kill the Messenger* in 2008. Once again, he was prepared. He studied the issues and the trends in pop culture and then turned them into humor.

Among the most important topics was the American presidential election, about which he entertained the crowd in Johannesburg, South Africa. It was an ideal subject for a foreign country with a mostly black population. After all, one of the two candidates was black Democrat Barack Obama. Rock expressed pride that a black man could reach the brink of the presidency in a nation that never would have considered voting for one a generation or two earlier.

Rock joked about the African name that the candidate inherited from his father. He claimed that the unique name made his success more unlikely and even sweeter to the American black community.

"Barack Obama!" he exclaimed. "A black man with a black name. I know it ain't that black here, but in America that's about as black as a name can get. Barack Obama! That's right next to [basketball star] Dikembe Mutombo.

"Barack don't let his blackness sneak up on you. If his name was Bob Jones or something, it might take you two or three weeks to realize he's black. But as soon as you hear 'Barack Obama' you expect to see a brother with a spear . . . just standing on top of a dead lion."

Rock touched upon a myriad of important social, economic, and political issues, such as racism, low-paying jobs, and the skyrocketing price of gas. But he also caused laughter with his takes on modern conveniences and frivolous topics, such as ringtones and bottled water.

His performance in *Kill the Messenger* did not garner the same level of critical acclaim that he achieved with *Bring the Pain* and *Bigger and Blacker* but not because of his material or delivery. The editing of the video put off some reviewers, which jumped from Rock performances in three different cities at various points in the show.

Some questioned whether Rock could be a success as a stand-up comedian in Europe. Rock was not one of them. Those who believed his material targeted mostly black audiences and would fail across the Atlantic were proven wrong. He announced several show dates in and around London that sold out in a day. It was sweet vindication for Rock, as he explained to *Rolling Stone* magazine reporter Bill Zehme.

"My old management—you'd tell somebody you're a black comedian and you want to play in London, they said, 'How about we book four more Detroit dates instead?' If you're going to be in the movie business, or any business nowadays, you have to establish yourself worldwide."

His next project was inspired by one of his daughters, who approached him one day with a curious question: "Daddy, why don't I have good hair?" Rock was taken aback by the question, which fell into the realm of self-image. Studies have shown that many black children, especially those of lower socio-economic groups, have lower self-images than white children of the same age.

The question sparked interest in Rock. He had considered the subject of black hairstyles fifteen years earlier during a convention in Atlanta in which black hair fashions were discussed. The specific subject was how black women with kinky hair go to great lengths to straighten it and give themselves a similar look to white women.

Rock recalled that convention and decided to create a film on the subject. He taped visits to beauty salons, barbershops, and wig manufacturers. He delved into how many African Americans were obsessed with having what they perceived as good hair. He explored how that affected the self-esteem and even finances of black people, particularly women.

The result was the 2009 documentary titled *Good Hair*. Just as Rock had done his entire career, he brought comedic relief to a touchy subject, at least to many African Americans. It received more positive reviews than his performances in fictional movies. It gave Rock a chance to be humorous off stage.

"[The documentary] does more than simply provide a social and cultural examination of black hair," wrote *Los Angeles Times* critic Greg Braxton in October 2009. "It also provides Rock with a film vehicle that effectively showcases his comic prowess, a goal that has proved largely elusive in films such as '*I Think I Love My Wife*' [and] '*Down to Earth*.' Interacting with salon customers, hair dealers and industry executives presents him as a more compelling film presence than his fictional [characters]."

Rock continued to focus on film. He produced and starred in a remake of a British comedy titled *Death at a Funeral* in 2010. Rock played an aspiring novelist and eldest son in a wealthy family whose father has died. His mother yearns for him and his wife to have a baby, but he wants only to write books like his younger brother.

The movie was a hit at the box office and received some good reviews. Included among them was a glowing report from Roger Ebert. Rock had been criticized for not performing in movie roles that best suited him. The rather raunchy humor in *Death at a Funeral* was more like what he been producing on stage since *Bring the Pain*.

By 2010, Rock had toiled as a stand-up comedian and writer, director, producer, and actor in both television and film. He would soon be performing in his first play. But his favorite job was still fatherhood.

Rock appeared for the thirty-fifth time on the *Oprah Winfrey Show* in 2011. She asked him to grade himself as a father. But he gave himself what amounted to an incomplete.

"It's the one job where you have to put 25 years in before you get your grade—you don't get midterms," he said. "Many a father or mother started off great, and then something happened and they fell off. Parenthood is a journey. It's a marathon. You don't get points for doing half the marathon."

One thing was certain. Rock was having a blast raising his two daughters.

"I think I'm getting better," he said. "I'm younger than the other parents, or younger *acting* anyway. I thought I was having fun when they were three, now they're nine and seven—fun! Now they can talk, and they've got opinions."

Family life had become extremely important to Rock. It was no wonder that his curiosity was piqued that same year when he learned all about his ancestry. What he discovered to his amazement extended back to slavery, the Civil War, and one very heroic man.

Chapter 7

EXPLORING HIS PAST AND FUTURE

A mong the subjects Chris Rock had joked about on stage over the years was slavery. But he was not attempting to make his audience laugh when he claimed that slavery, which ended nearly 150 years earlier, was still affecting African Americans and race relations today.

Rock might have suspected that his ancestors were slaves. Little could he have imagined that one of them was not only a slave for twenty-one years but blossomed into a successful politician just seven years later.

The revelation that brought Rock to tears occurred in 2011 on a PBS television show titled *African-American Lives*. Literary critic, educator, and scholar Henry Louis Gates, who hosted the program, sat down with Rock and explained what had been discovered about his American roots.

Rock knew about his maternal grandparents from Andrews, South Carolina. After all, Rock, too, was born in that area and lived there as a small child. His grandparents on his father's side were also from South Carolina.

The more Rock discovered about his ancestry, the more fascinated he became. When he learned about his mother's grandfather, he became particularly emotional. When he was told that Julius Caesar Tingman risked his life to fight with the U.S. Colored Troops against the Confederates at the end of the Civil War, Rock had to wipe tears streaming down his cheek. Rock was proud of Tingman, who had joined the battle just one month after being freed from slavery. After all, Tingman could have fled for the North or become a farmer, but he chose to fight for the freedom of others still enslaved.

"How does it feel to know that you have a direct ancestor who served in the Civil War?" Gates asked him.

"This whole thing is mind-blowing," Rock replied. "I knew *nothing* of this. . . . It's weird. If I had known this, there's a good chance I wouldn't have become a comedian. Until I lucked into a comedy club at age 20 just on a whim, I assumed I would pick up things for white people for the rest of my life. If I had known this, it would have taken away the inevitability that I was going to be nothing."

The pride Rock felt in his ancestry grew when he learned that Tingman was promoted from private to corporal within four months of joining the army, and he worked as a blacksmith. Rock was stunned to find out that Tingman was elected to the South Carolina state legislature in 1872, a revelation that nearly brought tears to his eyes again.

Rock might not have believed as a child that he would amount to much, but his mother never had any doubts. Rose Rock eventually landed a radio show in which she spoke about mothering and wrote a book titled *Mama Rock's Rules: Ten Lessons for Raising a Household of Successful Children*. She expressed her belief that her eldest son would be a success in life. She thought, however, that he would blossom into a famous writer rather than a comedian.

Perhaps the greatest compliment came unspoken from younger brother Tony Rock, who followed in his footsteps. The younger Rock emerged in the early

2000s as a successful comedian and actor. He first found success on stage in the Netherlands, but returned to New York after the turn of the century and became a regular at various comedy clubs. He later appeared in a few obscure films, including *C'Mon Man* (2012) and *Redemption of a Dog* (2012).

His older brother stopped touring as a stand-up comedian after *Kill the Messenger* in 2008. He was busy writing and acting in movies, but he wanted to explore a new avenue in his career. So in early 2011, he agreed to perform in his first play, the name of which contained an obscenity.

Rock's interest in plays was piqued in 2010 when he watched Oscar-winning black actor Denzel Washington in a Broadway production titled *Fences*. The performance moved him. He told producer Scott Rudin to find a script suitable to his talents, and he would accept a role. Rock added that he wanted to be part of an ensemble cast that took the spotlight off him. When Rudin presented him with a script for potentially his first Broadway play, he embraced the opportunity with enthusiasm.

It proved to be a learning experience for Rock. He was accustomed to performing on stage, but as a one-man show. Rock, the stand-up comedian, paced the stage like a caged lion. Rock, the play actor, was forced to share the stage with others. He had to focus not only on his lines, but also on his fellow actors. It required a wide focus.

Rock believed from the start all the hard work of learning a new talent would be worth it. He agreed with the old expression that variety is the spice of life.

"You get to the point where you think, 'I've done just about everything,'" he told Oprah Winfrey in 2011. "I've been blessed to have this career. I've been blessed to have this forum, and I should take complete advantage of it. Try everything, and if you don't like something you don't like it because you tried it, not because you dismissed it. . . . Your life can always be new."

Rock understood that this was different and more difficult than anything he had ever done professionally. But he also knew at age forty-six that he had matured as an entertainer. The frustration and anger that would have once ruined such a project for him was gone and replaced by quiet confidence. He understood that he was not *the* show, but merely *part* of the show.

The transition from film acting to stage acting was difficult for Rock. It required far more studying of his role and greater preparation. There were no second or third takes in performing live. He had to learn his lines and be able to recite them in front of an audience without mistakes. It was what he had done his entire career as a stand-up comedian, but the timing was different as he interacted with the other characters.

"This is not for the arrogant," he admitted to *New York Times* reporter Jon Caraminica. "You thought you were humble until you started doing a play. Ten years ago I'd have probably got fired already, or I'd have quit, and they'd have been happy I quit."

He was thrown right into the fire. The play about drug addiction and infidelity ran on Broadway, the New York epicenter of American theater. Rock played the role of Ralph D., a tragic, comic, and unsavory character.

Rock realized he was far less experienced as a stage actor than his fellow cast members. Most novices must toil for years in smaller venues and still never receive an opportunity to perform on Broadway. Considering he was being compared to fellow actors in the play, Rock received both positive and negative reviews for his performance. Some, like the following from *New York Magazine* critic Scott Brown, were mixed in their assessment of Rock: "The fact that the play's most dramatically consequential figure is also its most morally elusive probably doesn't help," Brown wrote. "The fact that this character is played by a rather chilly, rather remote comedian helps even less. I'm not saying Rock isn't funny: His specialties include flawless timing and devastating delivery, and on these scores, he delivers."

He delivered again in the 2012 comedy film titled *2 Days in New York*, which proved to be his most critically acclaimed performance. The movie was launched at the prestigious Sundance Film Festival, which is held annually in Park City, Utah.

Rock again took chances in accepting a role as a divorced father with a white girlfriend. They are living happily together until her uninhibited and unintentionally racist family members arrive from France. They spend two days in New York, testing the strength of the couple's relationship along the way.

In the midst of all the craziness, Rock's character plays the sanest member of the cast. To escape the others, he retreats into a private room to converse thoughtfully with a cardboard cutout of President Barack Obama.

The positive reviews earned by Rock and the movie placed him firmly on the road to achieving a professional goal. He had told noted talk-show host Charlie Rose in 2007 that he yearned to attract more rounded character roles from the greatest directors in the business. He had played one-dimensional characters in comedies universally panned early in his career. But performances such as those he gave in the Broadway play and *2 Days in New York* proved to

Rock and others that he was growing as both a serious and comedic actor.

Rock was changing as a person and as an entertainer. He was approaching fifty years old. Younger comedians began asking him for advice that he was happy to give. He realized that there were more obstacles on his path to greatness coming from the inner city of New York.

He embraced the chance to give others the benefit of his experience. He provided for them the same counsel given to him decades earlier by the veterans of stand-up comedy. He told them that they must move from the smaller cities to the show business centers of New York or Los Angeles. He stressed that they must be a student of comedy and yearn to be famous. And if they want to be like Rock, they can't shy away from creating controversy. Rock stirred up plenty of fireworks on July 4, 2012. While Americans were celebrating, Rock used Twitter to express his view of the holiday.

"Happy white peoples independence day the slaves weren't free but I'm sure they enjoyed fireworks," he tweeted.[1]

Rock understood that freedom of speech is an American ideal. He also knew that black people were in slavery when the nation was born on July 4, 1776, and nearly ninety years later. Many condemned him for his tweet. But others stated that Rock, who ignored the criticism, was merely offering the truth. Among them was fellow black comedian Elon James White.

"I find this Chris Rock backlash absolutely ridiculous," White said. "Really? Someone tells the truth and you mad? I'm American. I never claim otherwise. . . . But part of being American, to me, is that I have to acknowledge [everything] that comes with it. Basically some folks came over, stole [Indian] land, killed them, then started a country on the back of [black] people, while killing them, and then at some point they freed the slaves but then oppressed them and killed them some more.

"Do I have the ability to do things here that I wouldn't in some parts or the world? Yes. But my family paid the price for that in actual blood, sweat and tears. If more people were like Rock and acknowledged the truth maybe we'd be in a better place as a nation."

What Rock has shown he wants is a better nation and a better world. He is involved in a number of charities, many of which aid needy children in the United States and throughout the globe.

Rock has provided time and money for such organizations as the Andre Agassi Foundation for Education, which focus on at-risk and disadvantaged American kids. He has supported Champions for

Children and Elevate Hope Foundation, which is an advocate for abused children. He has helped many groups that feed, educate, and care for children and orphans in dire straits in Africa, such as Artists for a New South Africa, Raising Malawi, and UNICEF.

He has also been involved with the HollyRed Foundation, which provides relief for those with Parkinson's disease, and Music For Relief, which aids victims of natural disasters.

Rock has been greatly influenced by wife, Malaak. The couple has teamed up to create Journey for Change: Empowering Youth Through Global Service. In 2008, the organization collaborated with Malaak's Angel Rock Project and Salvation Army Southern African Territory to send at-risk children from New York City to South Africa for two weeks.

The kids, ages twelve to fifteen, volunteered to help orphans and other children in the townships of Diepsloot and Soweto. They worked in homes, schools, community centers, orphanages, clinics, and gardens. They also learned about the diverse culture in that country.

Rock expressed an appreciation for the project and his ability to help struggling children both from his old stomping ground in New York as well as in South Africa. Money was raised through an online auction.

"I didn't get the chance to travel outside my neighborhood until I was grown up and telling jokes," he said. "Journey for Change allows kids from my neighborhood in Brooklyn to go to South Africa to help those in need and then come back and advocate for change."[2]

Rock knew all about change. He had been growing as a person his entire life. He had grown into a well-rounded man and comedian. He had gone from living in a poor section of New York with no prospects to occupying a large mansion in Alpine, New Jersey, surrounded by other highly successful neighbors, such as music stars Mary J. Blige and Sean "Diddy" Combs. But if not for his courage to take a stand on stage, he never would have emerged as one of the greatest stand-up comics in American history. He understood at an early age that he needed to take chances to maximize his potential and separate himself from those who embraced other comedic styles.

"A lot of guys are great, but they don't want to hit *hard*," he told Scott Raab of *Esquire* magazine. "To hit like (boxing champion Mike Tyson) up there. . . . It's hard to hit homers. I try to hit homers. I'm not a singles hitter. I'm swinging like (baseball slugger Gary Sheffield) every time. As *hard* as I can."

Trying to hit "home runs" on stage is risky. Because when you go for the big laugh and get no laugh at all, that's the toughest moment for a comedian. Rock has always been willing to take chances because that makes success even more rewarding.

"It's all about the jokes at the end of the day," he told David Bennun of *Life* magazine. "The only reaction that frightens me is people not laughing. It's extraordinary to me when you get a laugh. That you can go in front of a bunch of people you never met before, you can say some stuff and they all laugh in unison—*that's* amazing. It's a *miracle*."

People not laughing? It seems almost impossible that Chris Rock should ever be frightened about that.

CHRONOLOGY

1966—Born on February 7 in Andrews, South Carolina, to Rose and Julius Rock.

1972—Family moves to New York.

1983—Drops out of mostly white high school and begins performing at comedy clubs around New York.

1986—Befriends comic hero Eddie Murphy at The Comic Strip comedy club.

1987—Murphy signs him up for HBO show *Uptown Comedy Express* and for bit part as parking attendant in film *Beverly Hills Cop 2*.

1988—Shaken by death of father, Julius.

1990—Lands spot as cast member of iconic comedy skit program *Saturday Night Live*.

1991—Plays role of crack addict in movie *New Jack City*.

1993—Lack of opportunity motivates him to leave *Saturday Night Live*; briefly works on cast of TV hit *In Living Color*; meets future wife Malaak Compton.

1994—Stars on HBO with stand-up *Big Ass Jokes*.

1996—Performance on HBO special *Bring the Pain* catapults him to stardom; marries Malaak Compton on November 23.

1997—Lands HBO talk show titled the *Chris Rock Show* and it runs until 2000; authors first book, *Rock This!*; receives two Emmy Awards for *Bring the Pain.*

1998—Lands feature role in *Lethal Weapon 4.*

1999—HBO special *Bigger and Blacker* earns critical acclaim; hosts MTV Video Music Awards.

2001—Produces and stars in movies *Down to Earth* and *Pootie Tang.*

2002—Serves as executive producer of TV series *The Hughleys*; birth of first daughter, Lola.

2003—Writes, produces, and stars in film *Head of State.*

2004—HBO stand-up special *Never Scared* gains critical acclaim; birth of second daughter, Zahra.

2005—Popular, well-received TV show *Everybody Hates Chris* is launched and runs until 2009; hosts Academy Awards.

2007—Produces, directs, and stars in film *I Think I Love My Wife.*

2008—HBO special *Kill the Messenger* features stand-up routines in Johannesburg (South Africa), London, and New York.

2009—Comment from daughter results in highly acclaimed documentary *Good Hair*.

2010—Stars in film *Death at a Funeral*.

2012—Receives positive reviews for performance in movie *2 Days in New York*; lands role in Broadway play, which proves to be challenging learning experience.

DISCOGRAPHY & FILMOGRAPHY

Selected Films

Grown Ups 2 (2013)

What to Expect When You're Expecting (2012)

2 Days in New York (2011)

Grown Ups (2010)

Death at a Funeral (2010)

Bee Movie (2007)

I Think I Love My Wife (2007)

Madagascar (2005)

The Longest Yard (2005)

Head of State (2003)

Bad Company (2002)

Pootie Tang (2001)

Down to Earth (2001)

Dogma (1999)

Lethal Weapon 4 (1998)

Beverly Hills Ninja (1997)

CB4 (1993)

Boomerang (1992)

New Jack City (1991)

Beverly Hills Cop II (1987)

Discography

Never Scared (2005)

Bigger & Blacker (1999)

Roll With the New (1997)

Born Suspect (1991)

Selected Television

Kill the Messenger (2008)

Everybody Hates Chris (2005–2009)

Never Scared (2004)

Bigger & Blacker (2000)

The Chris Rock Show (1997–2000)

Bring the Pain (1996)

Big Ass Jokes (1994)

Saturday Night Live (1990–1993)

CHAPTER NOTES

Chapter 1: Inspiring a Comic Genius

1. David Keeps, "Chris Rock Steps Up." *Best Life*, April 2007. Volume 4, Issue 3.

2. "Chris Rock on Gun Control," *YouTube.com*, May 13, 2008, <http://www.youtube.com/watch?v=OuX-nFmL0II> (August 21, 2012).

Chapter 2: Tough Love, Tough Childhood

1. Eddie M. Tafoya, *Icons of African American Comedy* (Santa Barbara, Calif.: ABC-CLIO, 2011), p. 221.

2. "Comedy's Dirtiest Dozen 1988 Chris Rock," *YouTube .com*, August 17, 2008, <http://www.youtube.com/watch?v=QruwekfAJwc> (August 23, 2012).

Chapter 3: Birth of a Superstar

1. Chris Rock, *Rock This!* (New York: Hyperion Books, 2000), p. 48.

Chapter 4: New Wife, New Life

1. "Chris Rock on Racism," *YouTube.com*, April 19, 2009, <http://www.youtube.com/watch?v=MdQg7jTXUt8> (September 6, 2012).

Chapter 6: Loving *Everybody Hates Chris*

1. David Keeps, "Chris Rock Steps Up." *Best Life*, April 2007. Volume 4, Issue 3.

Chapter 7: Exploring His Past and Future

1. Gael Fashingbauer Cooper, "Chris Rock draws fire for July 4 tweet about 'white peoples independence day,'" *NBC News*, July 5, 2012, <http://todayentertainment.today.com/_news/2012/07/05/12578174-chris-rock-draws-fire-for-july-4-tweet-about-white-peoples-independence-day?lite> (September 13, 2012).

2. "Meet Chris Rock and Malaak Compton-Rock for Charity," *Look to the Stars: The World of Celebrity Giving*, July 8, 2010, <http://www.looktothestars.org/news/4713-meet-chris-rock-and-malaak-compton-rock-for-charity> (September 14, 2012).

GLOSSARY

affirmative action—Giving preferential treatment in hiring to a race or gender to even out past discrimination.

busing—The act of moving students to schools outside their districts for the purpose of providing equal educations.

cast—A group of actors working on the same project.

critic—A person who offers an opinion on any kind of performance.

director—Someone who supervises the making of a film, TV show, or play.

discrimination—Negative treatment of somebody, usually based on race, gender, or religion.

documentary—A film re-creating or making a statement about an actual event.

Emmy—An award given annually to top performances in television.

Oscar—An award given annually to top performers in film.

pop culture—Related to the world of entertainment.

producer—A person responsible for the financial and administrative duties of any production.

review—A written or spoken critique, usually of a movie, play, or TV show.

routine—A bit performed on stage by a comedian.

script—The written words and actions followed by actors.

sitcom—A form of TV entertainment known as a situation comedy.

stand-up—A stage comedian or his or her routine.

FURTHER READING

Books

Robson, David. *Chris Rock*. Philadelphia: Mason Crest, 2009.

Todd, Anne M. *Chris Rock: Comedian and Actor*. New York: Chelsea House, 2006.

Internet Addresses

Biography.com: Chris Rock
<http://www.biography.com/people/chris-rock-9542306>

IMDb: Chris Rock
<http://www.imdb.com/name/nm0001674/>

INDEX